# 101
# Quips and Quotes

## That will Charge and Change your Life

---

### ADA ADELEKE-KELANI

WestBow Press books may be ordered through booksellers or by contacting:

WestBow Press
A Division of Thomas Nelson & Zondervan
1663 Liberty Drive
Bloomington, IN 47403
www.westbowpress.com
1 (866) 928-1240

Because of the dynamic nature of the Internet, any web addresses or links contained in this book may have changed since publication and may no longer be valid. The views expressed in this work are solely those of the author and do not necessarily reflect the views of the publisher, and the publisher hereby disclaims any responsibility for them.

Any people depicted in stock imagery provided by Getty Images are models, and such images are being used for illustrative purposes only.
Certain stock imagery © Getty Images.

Scripture quotations marked (GNT) are from the Good News Translation in Today's English Version-Second Edition Copyright © 1992 by American Bible Society. Used by Permission.

ISBN: 978-1-9736-6833-6 (sc)
ISBN: 978-1-9736-6834-3 (e)

Library of Congress Control Number: 2019908994

Print information available on the last page.

WestBow Press rev. date: 08/28/2019

WestBow
PRESS®
A DIVISION OF THOMAS NELSON
& ZONDERVAN

# Dedication

**This book is dedicated to God**
Who has blessed and continues to inspire me with
quips and quotes
that have charged and changed my life...and the lives of others around me.

# Acknowledgement

There are so many people who contributed to this book starting with my parents (of blessed memory). Though I really miss both my parents, I am profoundly grateful for all that they showed and taught me. As I think about them, I know that it is natural to be sad having lost them when we did however, I am also glad and incredibly grateful to God that my brothers and I were blessed with such parents.

Heartfelt thanks go to 5 very special men in my life…in the order that they came into my life:
My brothers, Chuma and Emeka have been a source of influence and inspiration for this book – in so many more ways than they know. Together, we are an ACE in life.

My husband, my One & Only for life…he is my partner in progress and purpose fulfillment. He set the ball rolling by challenging and encouraging me to write a book. Our sons, Obasegun and Ibunkunolu, who in their unique ways are evidence of our progress and purpose fulfillment.

I cannot but acknowledge: My coach, Jacquie Stephens, who encouraged me fulfill my dream of writing a book; My dear friend, Chinyere Almona who helped me tremendously – encouraging me each step of the way and helped me edit and organize this book; and My "guide" Kim Staflund, who shared ideas on how to publish my books.

This book will not be complete without acknowledging you my readers; knowing that as you read and share this book it will charge and change your life and others' lives is a privilege and a blessing I do not take for granted. Thank you.

Blessings,
Ada

# Contents

# Introduction

Our world is the result of the Word of God. From the creation of the world till eternity, words will always create the "world" you live in. It is up to you to decide which words you will adopt and adapt your life to.

I was inspired to write this book to share some words – quips and quotes – that have charged and changed my life. We have more power to change our lives than we realize.

You will notice that I have written this book in first and third person as I did my best to retain the quips and quotes in their original format. I could go on and on about how words directly from God or through others to me and even from God through me to others have charged and changed my life. However, I would rather let you go on and read this book.

I pray they have similar impact in your life and in the lives of those who come in contact with you.

# 1

## Christian Living

1.  I choose to obey God, so that my posterity will enjoy prosperity. See Deuteronomy 6.

2.  Living independent of God does not diminish God in any way.

3.  Daring to be independent of God is signing up for an incomplete life.

4.	You don't need to be the greatest to do great things – you just need a Great God.

5.	In times like these when options abound, total and timely obedience to God is not an option. It's an obligation you fulfill for your own good.

6.	Live transparently so others can see God's light in and through your life.

7.	When there is an upset in our lives, it may be God's set up for us to step up to our next level.

8. Everyone has a right to (express) their opinion about me. I have a right to ignore others' opinions of me and a responsibility to align myself to God's opinion of me.

9. No matter how loud man's applause is, God's approval is all you need in life.

10. The fact that you think that you haven't done anything wrong doesn't mean that you have done everything right...focus on doing right...

# 2

# Marriage and Family Matters

11. The best marriages are where each spouse gives 100% irrespective of what they are receiving (or not receiving) as the case may be.

12. When you are having challenges in marriage, husbands look back to why you asked your wife to marry you; wives look back to why you said "Yes," and stick with each other.

13. Funny how we say that "opposites attract", marry someone who's different from us and later get upset that they haven't changed to be like us. Always remember the initial attraction...and stay married for life.

14. In marriage, each spouse shines brighter as you take the time to support & 'polish' each other. Do not be a 'polish remover' to your spouse.

15. The fact that your spouse seems to be "low-maintenance" does not mean that they are "no-maintenance". Take the time to care and serve each other in little and big ways.

16. We should learn to listen to our spouse with our heart not with our head. To do this effectively, be silent... and truly listen. Remember that the same letters are used to spell 'LISTEN' and 'SILENT.'

17. No matter what you and your spouse may disagree about, always agree that your marriage is more important than any disagreement.

18. Your spouse's infertility is not a valid reason for infidelity, nor is their infidelity. There's no valid reason for infidelity.

19. Children are a by-product of marriage and must never be the "bye-producer." Your children must never come between you and your spouse.

20. The best mothers don't smother or spoil their children. The best mothers mold and are role-models for their children.

21. We should always give our dearest our best selves and the rest to the rest of the world – not the other way around.

FAMILY
* WHERE *
LIFE BEGINS
* AND *
Love
NEVER ENDS

22. If you have faith in God, pass it on to your children so they have it too before you pass on.

23. Your family is your family for life…so always speak life to them.

24. Live in such a way that whatever you leave behind lives on to God's glory.

25. Enjoy every minute you have with your family and friends so you're not full of regret when they leave.

# 3

# Living a purpose-filled life

26. There's a price for every prize. When you pay the right price, you'll get the desired prize.

27. Turn your stumbling blocks into stepping stones…make them help not hurt you.

28. Convert every failure into a stepping stone and avoid letting any of your successes become a stumbling block.

29. The fact that life is as fragile as a raw egg means that you can still fulfill your purpose in life as an "omelette" if you feel a bit cracked...

30. The best lives are lived on purpose for a purpose.

31. When you discover and decide to walk in your purpose be aware that there will be people who want to put you down, pull you back or push you under...don't let them distract or detract you.

32. The best punctuation mark after a success or failure is a question mark. Ask yourself "What next?" then continue your quest to accomplish more.

33. To die empty, you need to live and give fully each day.

34. People should be glad, not sad, wherever you go and are. People should be sad, not glad, whenever you go.

35. Don't talk because you can speak, talk because you have something worthwhile to say.

36. If you don't use it, you lose it. Use your gifts to be a blessing so you don't lose them.

37. Ensure that you don't allow your gifts become dormant, otherwise, you may become or be treated as a "doormat."

38. When you live in denial, you delay your progress and success.

39. I celebrate all my "baby steps." When you celebrate small successes, you'll eventually have major milestones to celebrate.

40. Live your life by choice not by chance.

# 4

## Self-Management

41. Have the "Oxygen Mask" mentality. Self-care is not selfishness. Self-only is selfishness. Remember that the Bible says, "you must love your neighbor as you love *yourself*." (Luke 12:33b - GNT)

42. You can share without caring but you can't care without sharing.

43. If what is desirable is not available, make what's available desirable.

44. Setting boundaries help you keep your priorities on track.

45. If you don't know how to rest, a life of stress is guaranteed (see Mark 6:31)

46. When you overstretch yourself, stress, strain and snapping is sure to follow.

47. You don't have any control over others' opinion of you...focus and act on what God thinks about you.

Every Accomplishment Starts With the Decision to *Try.*

48. Self-awareness and acceptance are the key to self-mastery.

49. Failures are a period in time but should never put a period (full stop) to your aiming higher.

50. Age is a number so it's good to age gradually, better to age gracefully, and best to age gratefully.

51. Being an "open book" doesn't mean that every page of the book is open at the same time. People should get to know you better as they spend more time with you.

52. Be careful of giving people a piece of your mind so you don't "run out of mind" and peace.

53. Prosperity is best enjoyed when there is peace.

54. Learning to say "No" without feeling guilty gives you the opportunity to say "Yes" to other things with pleasure not pressure.

55. Your words should engender life not endanger people's lives.

# CHAPTER

# 5

# Leadership

56. Good leaders lead themselves first not lead with self first.

57. Good leaders groom staff. Great leaders groom others and make room for them to bloom.

58. The best leaders lead with their heart not their heads...and lift a hand to help too.

59. Watch yourself even if (and when) no one is watching.

60. Empowered people empower others – irrespective of gender.

61. How low are you willing to stoop to rise higher? The fact that you start low doesn't mean that you'll stay low…except you refuse to grow.

62. The fact that something is difficult doesn't mean that it is impossible.

63. Once dead you won't matter so ensure that you matter while you are alive.

64. It's important to know who you are and equally important to know who you're not. The latter will help you set boundaries for you to live fully in.

65. Asking for help is evidence of wisdom. Receiving help is evidence of strength. The weak and unwise never ask for or receive help.

# 6

# Thanksgiving

66. Our prayers of thanksgiving should outnumber our prayers of asking.

67. When you give God thanks, He gives you more reasons to give thanks.

68. Thanksgiving must be a permanent part of our daily living not just a day in our lives...

69. Thanksgiving is a day a year – Thanks-living is a way of life all year.

70. Gratitude is the best attitude that leads to a higher altitude and you don't need aptitude for it.

71. In a world full of words, "Please" and "Thank you" are words you should use everyday.

спасибо
谢谢
GRACIAS
THANK YOU
ありがとうございました MERCI
DANKE धन्यवाद
شُكراً OBRIGADO

72. No matter what you forget or discard of what your parents taught you, never discard saying "Please" and "Thank you".

73. Saying "Please" and "Thank you" can open (more) doors for you with ease

74. Mention it - say "Thank you". Don't be misled by those who say, "Don't mention it." Jesus never said, "Don't mention it." He actually wondered why it was not mentioned – see Luke 17: 11-19.

75. Thanksgiving is a state of the heart, not a state of the mouth. At the heart of the matter, it's a matter of the heart.

# Life and Relationships

76. The friends you choose "choose" your future.

77. Diversity is by default; Inclusion is by design.

78. Equality is important, but equity is more valuable…we're each unique and should be treated equitably not equally.

79. The way you treat yourself, teaches others how to treat you. Treat yourself with love and respect.

80. If you keep sweeping things under the carpet, one day you'll trip over the bump you have created.

81. Every sigh is a sign that a song is coming your way…

82. It has been said that common sense is common. I have found that the lack of common sense is even more common.

83. We should be gracious givers and grateful receivers. Since it is more blessed to give than to receive, give others the opportunity of being blessed.

84. If you believe that you don't have enough to spare and share with others, you'll never have enough to spare and share.

85. Seek and use every opportunity to be good to everyone.

86. We spend 80% of our time awake at work so work must be fun or fulfilling otherwise it's a miserable way to live your life.

87. Your junk could be another person's jewel.

88. If you can "dish" it, you should be ready to eat it...when "dished out" to you.

89. The best way to deal with offences is "put the fence off"...and forgive.

90. Forgiveness is a gift you give to yourself and it usually comes wrapped in offence

# CHAPTER

# 8

## Time for Change

91. Get "comfortable" being out of your Comfort Zone so you can grow.

92. You cannot grow if you refuse to change.

93. The best way to start anything in life is to start small. The "worst" way to stay is to stay small. Growth is evidence of life.

94. Watch your words, they are seeds...you'll see what you say.

95. Move beyond barely surviving and to truly thriving.

96. It's good to have great wishes and great to do the work required to make your wishes come true.

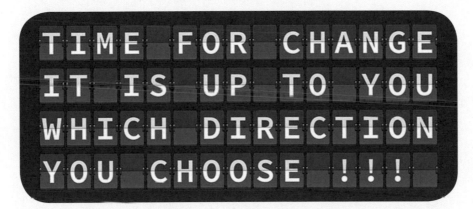

TIME FOR CHANGE
IT IS UP TO YOU
WHICH DIRECTION
YOU CHOOSE !!!

97. Your past will only pester you if you refuse to move past it.

98. Your glory is in your story...don't forget your history but don't live there.

99. Leave your past behind – it's past and live fully in your present, for the future that awaits you.

100. The fact that you've messed up doesn't mean that you need to live in that mess.

101. Getting better daily is the best way to live.

# 11 Bonus Quips and Quotes

1. Too many people summarize their blessings and detail their problems Rather, count your blessings and summarize your problems. – 'Leke Kelani

2. When you praise God with reckless abandon, He blesses you with reckless abandon. – 'Leke Kelani

3. Don't go where God has not sent you. Don't stay where God will not support you. – 'Leke Kelani

4. If you don't like your output, check your input. If you don't like your harvest, check your seed. – 'Leke Kelani

5.  Establish godly family values that will outlive you. – 'Leke Kelani

6.  Expose yourself to the Word of God not to the words of the world. – 'Leke Kelani

7.  Your faith is seen in the actions you take. – 'Leke Kelani

8.  Our actions amplify our convictions. – 'Leke Kelani

9. You can believe from today till forever, nothing will change until you take action to change it. – 'Leke Kelani

10. It is only the Great God that can make a man great and keep him great. – 'Leke Kelani

# Conclusion

Putting this book together reminded me of the age-old adage that "the journey of a thousand miles, starts with a step."

The first step is usually what it takes to encourage us to take the next step and the next.

It is my hope and prayer that after going through these quotes and quips that your next step will be to apply them in your life and share them with others that you care about.

As for me, my next step is to change more lives and start on my next book…

Printed in the United States
By Bookmasters